Popsicles

A Simple Popsicle Cookbook for Making Delicious Popsicles

By
BookSumo Press

Published by
http://www.booksumo.com

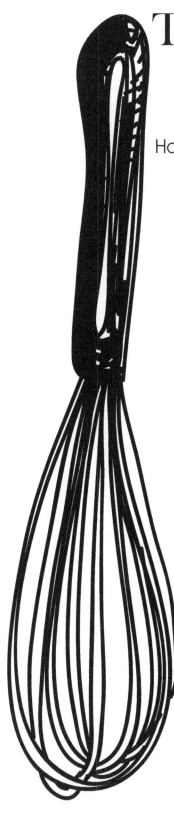

Table of Contents

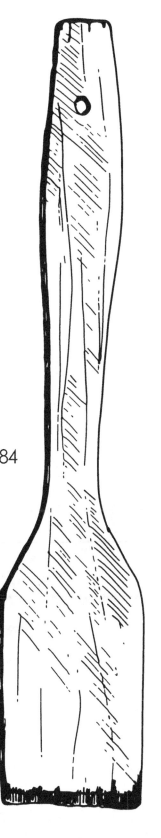

Fudge
Paletas 101

Prep Time: 10 mins
Total Time: 10 mins

Servings per Recipe: 1

Calories	165.3
Fat	5.8 g
Cholesterol	19.3 mg
Sodium	67.1 mg
Carbohydrates	24.9 g
Protein	3.7 g

Ingredients
1/2 C. sugar
2 tbsp. cornstarch
2 tbsp. Hershey's cocoa powder
2 1/2 C. milk
1 tsp. vanilla
1 tbsp. butter

Directions
1. In a pan, add the milk, sugar, cocoa, cornstarch over medium heat and cook until mixture becomes thick, stirring frequently.
2. Remove from the heat and stir in the butter and vanilla until smooth.
3. Transfer the mixture into Popsicle molds evenly.
4. Now, insert 1 Popsicle stick into each mold and place in the freezer until set completely.
5. Carefully, remove the popsicles from molds and enjoy.

CHOCOLATE
Melon Pops

 Prep Time: 30 mins

Total Time: 11 h 30 mins

Servings per Recipe: 24

Calories	135.9
Fat	1.8 g
Cholesterol	0.2 mg
Sodium	13.5 mg
Carbohydrates	30.9 g
Protein	1.4 g

Ingredients

1 small watermelon, seedless
1 C. sugar
1/2 C. mini chocolate chip
2 pints lime sherbet, softened

Directions

1. In a food processor, add 10 C. of the watermelon pulp and sugar in batches and pulse until smooth.
2. Through a mesh strainer, strain the puree into a bowl.
3. Cover the bowl and place in the freezer for about 3 hours.
4. Remove from the freezer and stir in the chocolate chips.
5. Transfer the mixture into 24 (3-oz.) disposable cups about 1/2-inch away from the rim.
6. Arrange the cups into 2 shallow baking dishes and freeze for about 2 hours.
7. Place the sherbet on top of each cup evenly and with the edge of a butter knife, smooth the top surface.
8. With a plastic wrap, cover each cup.
9. With a knife, cut small slit in the center of each wrap.
10. Now, insert 1 Popsicle stick into the slit of each wrap so it reaches to the bottom.
11. Place in the freezer for about 8 hours or up to 2 days.
12. Remove the cups from the freezer and keep aside at room temperature for about 1 minute.
13. Carefully, remove the popsicles from cups and enjoy.

How to Make a
Creamy Popsicle

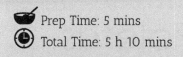 Prep Time: 5 mins

Total Time: 5 h 10 mins

Servings per Recipe: 4

Calories	69.2
Fat	1.9 g
Cholesterol	7.9 mg
Sodium	28.6 mg
Carbohydrates	11.5 g
Protein	2.1 g

Ingredients
1 C. plain yogurt
1 C. fresh fruit (blueberries, strawberries, cherries, etc.)
2 tbsp. honey
4 wooden popsicle sticks
4 paper C., 5 oz. size
aluminum foil

Directions
1. In a food processor, add the fruit, yogurt and honey and pulse until slightly smooth.
2. Place the fruit mixture into the paper cups about 3/4 of full.
3. With a foil piece, cover each cup.
4. With a knife, cut small slit in the center of each foil piece.
5. Now, insert 1 Popsicle stick into the slit of each foil piece so it reaches to the bottom.
6. Freeze for about 5 hours.
7. Carefully, remove the popsicles from cups and enjoy.

LIME BERRY
Paletas

Prep Time: 5 mins
Total Time: 5 mins

Servings per Recipe: 24
Calories   48.0
Fat   0.1 g
Cholesterol   0.0 mg
Sodium   1.3 mg
Carbohydrates   12.2 g
Protein   0.2 g

Ingredients
1 C. mashed strawberry
1/2 C. water
3-4 tbsp. sugar
juice of half lime

Directions
1. In a bowl, add all ingredients and mix until well combined.
2. Transfer the mixture into Popsicle molds evenly.
3. Now, insert 1 Popsicle stick into each mold and place in the freezer until set completely.
4. Carefully, remove the popsicles from molds and enjoy.

Leila's
Favorite

🥣 Prep Time: 15 mins
🕐 Total Time: 3 h 15 mins

Servings per Recipe: 10
Calories	454.4
Fat	15.5 g
Cholesterol	0.9 mg
Sodium	318.7 mg
Carbohydrates	73.2 g
Protein	8.6 g

Ingredients

5 bananas, just ripe, peeled and cut in half
10 wooden popsicle sticks
1 C. peanuts, finely chopped
3 C. chocolate syrup, dark hard shell

Directions

1. Carefully, insert 1 Popsicle sticks into each banana half.
2. Dip each banana half into the chocolate syrup and then, coat with peanuts.
3. Place in the freezer for about 3 hours.
4. Enjoy chilled.

JAMAICAN STYLE
Pops

Prep Time: 5 mins
Total Time: 4 h 5 mins

Servings per Recipe: 8
Calories   155.0
Fat   6.0 g
Cholesterol   0.0 mg
Sodium   14.1 mg
Carbohydrates   25.3 g
Protein   0.5 g

Ingredients
1 1/4 C. pineapple juice
1 C. coconut milk
1 1/2 tbsp. Splenda sugar substitute

Directions
1. In a bowl, add all the ingredients and mix until splenda is dissolved completely.
2. Transfer the mixture into Popsicle molds evenly.
3. Now, insert 1 Popsicle stick into each mold and place in the freezer overnight.
4. Carefully, remove the popsicles from molds and enjoy.

Red and Orange
Paletas

🥣 Prep Time: 5 mins
🕐 Total Time: 5 mins

Servings per Recipe: 1
Calories   31.1
Fat   0.0 g
Cholesterol   0.0 mg
Sodium   0.7 mg
Carbohydrates   7.7 g
Protein   0.2 g

Ingredients

1 1/2 C. diced watermelon
1 C. orange juice
1 C. water
1/4 C. sugar

Directions

1. In a bowl, add the orange juice and sugar and mix until sugar dissolves completely.
2. In a food processor, add the sugar mixture and remaining ingredients and pulse until well combined.
3. Transfer the mixture into Popsicle molds evenly.
4. Now, insert 1 Popsicle stick into each mold and place in the freezer until set completely.
5. Carefully, remove the popsicles from molds and enjoy.

POET
Pops

 Prep Time: 5 mins
Total Time: 3 h 5 mins

Servings per Recipe: 8
Calories	28.5
Fat	0.0 g
Cholesterol	0.0 mg
Sodium	0.6 mg
Carbohydrates	7.2 g
Protein	0.0 g

Ingredients
3/4 C. fresh strawberries, hulled
1/4 C. sugar
1/2 C. water

Directions
1. In a food processor, add all the ingredients and pulse until well combined.
2. Transfer the mixture into Popsicle molds evenly.
3. Now, insert 1 Popsicle stick into each mold and place in the freezer for about 3 hours.
4. Carefully, remove the popsicles from molds and enjoy.

Polynesian
Pops

Prep Time: 20 mins
Total Time: 6 h 20 mins

Servings per Recipe: 6
Calories	161.4
Fat	6.1 g
Cholesterol	0.0 mg
Sodium	13.7 mg
Carbohydrates	27.1 g
Protein	0.7 g

Ingredients
1 1/4 C. mangoes, chopped
3/4 C. coconut milk
1-2 tbsp. sugar
1 tbsp. lime juice

Directions
1. In a food processor, add all the ingredients and pulse until smooth.
2. Transfer the mixture into Popsicle molds evenly.
3. Now, insert 1 Popsicle stick into each mold and place in the freezer until set completely.
4. Carefully, remove the popsicles from molds and enjoy.

SIMPLE
Spring Pops

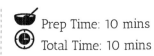 Prep Time: 10 mins
Total Time: 10 mins

Servings per Recipe: 6
Calories	106.9
Fat	2.5 g
Cholesterol	9.9 mg
Sodium	36.2 mg
Carbohydrates	17.2 g
Protein	3.4 g

Ingredients
16 oz. vanilla yogurt
2 tsp. vanilla
1 (6 oz.) cans frozen orange juice
concentrate

Directions
1. In a food processor, add all the ingredients and pulse until smooth.
2. Transfer the mixture into Popsicle molds evenly.
3. Now, insert 1 Popsicle stick into each mold and place in the freezer until set completely.
4. Carefully, remove the popsicles from molds and enjoy.

Cookie
Popsicles 101

🥣 Prep Time: 15 mins
🕐 Total Time: 3 h 15 mins

Servings per Recipe: 8
Calories   247.8
Fat   18.7 g
Cholesterol   56.3 mg
Sodium   129.3 mg
Carbohydrates   19.0 g
Protein   2.2 g

Ingredients
4 oz. cream cheese
1/2 C. confectioners' sugar
1 C. heavy whipping cream
10 Oreo cookies

Directions
1. In the bowl of a mixer with whisk attachment, add the confectioners' sugar and cream cheese and beat on medium speed until smooth.
2. Gradually, add the heavy cream and beat on low speed until smooth.
3. Freeze the bowl for about 45 minutes, mixing often.
4. Chop 5 Oreo cookies roughly.
5. In the bottom of Popsicle molds, divide the chopped Oreo cookies and top with the cream cheese mixture evenly.
6. Now, insert 1 Popsicle stick into each mold and freeze for about 4 hours.
7. In a food processor, add the remaining 5 Oreo cookies and pulse until a fine crumbs like mixture is formed.
8. Carefully, remove the popsicles from cups and coat each Popsicle with the Oreo crumb evenly.
9. Enjoy.

10-MINUTE
Paletas

Prep Time: 10 mins
Total Time: 10 mins

Servings per Recipe: 4
Calories   164.9
Fat   0.5 g
Cholesterol   2.4 mg
Sodium   433.2 mg
Carbohydrates   35.8 g
Protein   5.1 g

Ingredients

3 1/2 oz. instant banana pudding mix
2 C. skim milk
1 banana, pieces

Directions

1. In a bowl, add the milk and pudding mix and mix until well combined.
2. Add the banana pieces and gently, stir to combine.
3. Transfer the mixture into Popsicle molds evenly.
4. Now, insert 1 Popsicle stick into each mold and place in the freezer until firm completely.
5. Carefully, remove the popsicles from molds and enjoy.

Hubby's Favorite
Paletas

🥣 Prep Time: 10 mins
🕐 Total Time: 10 mins

Servings per Recipe: 4
Calories   37.3
Fat   1.9 g
Cholesterol   7.9 mg
Sodium   28.1 mg
Carbohydrates   2.8 g
Protein   2.1 g

Ingredients
1 C. fruit flavored yogurt
1/3 C. pureed fruit
1 tbsp. sugar

Directions
1. In a bowl, add all the ingredients and mix until well combined.
2. Transfer the mixture into Popsicle molds evenly.
3. Now, insert 1 Popsicle stick into each mold and place in the freezer for about 6 hours.
4. Carefully, remove the popsicles from molds and enjoy.

CREAMY
Italian Paletas

Prep Time: 10 mins
Total Time: 4 h 10 mins

Servings per Recipe: 8
Calories	78.1
Fat	1.5 g
Cholesterol	5.9 mg
Sodium	21.9 mg
Carbohydrates	15.2 g
Protein	1.7 g

Ingredients
1/3 C. honey
1 1/2 C. plain yogurt
1 C. chopped strawberries
1 tsp. vanilla

Directions
1. In a food processor, add all the ingredients and pulse until smooth.
2. Transfer the mixture into Dixie cups and place in the freezer for about 4 hours.
3. Now, insert 1 Popsicle stick into each cup.
4. Place in the freezer for about 4 hours.
5. Carefully, remove the popsicles from cups and enjoy.

Sweet Lime Pops

🥣 Prep Time: 10 mins
🕐 Total Time: 10 mins

Servings per Recipe: 8
Calories   24.9
Fat   0.5 g
Cholesterol   1.9 mg
Sodium   8.1 mg
Carbohydrates   4.9 g
Protein   0.5 g

Ingredients

440 g crushed pineapple in natural juice
1/2 C. natural yoghurt
1 lime, juice of
2 tbsp. brown sugar
8 wooden icy pole sticks

Directions

1. In a bowl, add all the ingredients and with a stick blender, blend until well combined and smooth.
2. Transfer the mixture into Popsicle molds evenly.
3. Now, insert 1 Popsicle stick into each mold and place in the freezer overnight.
4. Carefully, remove the popsicles from molds and enjoy.

HOT
Cucumber Pops

Prep Time: 5 mins
Total Time: 8 h 5 mins

Servings per Recipe: 6
Calories   97.5
Fat   0.1 g
Cholesterol   0.0 mg
Sodium   1.4 mg
Carbohydrates   25.2 g
Protein   0.4 g

Ingredients
3 C. cucumbers, peeled, chunks
2/3 C. sugar
1/3 C. lemon juice
1 jalapeño chile

Directions
1. In a food processor, add all the ingredients and pulse until smooth.
2. Through a fine strainer, strain the mixture into a bowl.
3. Transfer the mixture into Popsicle molds evenly.
4. Now, insert 1 Popsicle stick into each mold and place in the freezer for about 9 hours.
5. Carefully, remove the popsicles from molds and enjoy.

Hannah's
Cookout Pops

Prep Time: 5 mins
Total Time: 4 h 5 mins

Servings per Recipe: 6
Calories	114.9
Fat	4.3 g
Cholesterol	15.9 mg
Sodium	88.3 mg
Carbohydrates	14.1 g
Protein	5.0 g

Ingredients
3 C. vanilla yogurt
red food coloring
white food coloring
blue food coloring

wax paper
6 sugar ice cream cones
6 wooden popsicle sticks

Directions
1. In a bowl, add 1/2 C. of the yogurt and red food coloring and mix well.
2. In another bowl, add 1 1/2 C. of the yogurt and blue food coloring and mix well.
3. Fold 6 (12-inch) square wax paper sheets into triangles.
4. Wrap 1 wax paper triangle around each sugar cone tightly.
5. Then, carefully place each paper cone inside the sugar cone.
6. Place about 1 tbsp. of the red yogurt into each cone, followed by 2 tbsp. of the plain yogurt and 3 tbsp. of the blue yogurt.
7. Now, insert 1 Popsicle stick into each cone.
8. Place in the freezer for about 4 hours.
9. Carefully, remove the popsicles from each cone and enjoy.

ST LOUIS
Blueberry Pops

Prep Time: 10 mins
Total Time: 6 h 10 mins

Servings per Recipe: 8
Calories   58.7
Fat   2.2 g
Cholesterol   8.2 mg
Sodium   29.3 mg
Carbohydrates   8.0 g
Protein   2.3 g

Ingredients
1 pint fresh blueberries
1 C. vanilla yogurt
1 C. milk
sugar, to taste

Directions
1. In a food processor, add all the ingredients and pulse until smooth.
2. Transfer the mixture into 5-oz. paper cups evenly.
3. With a piece of foil, cover each cup.
4. With a knife, cut small slit in the center of each wrap.
5. Now, insert 1 Popsicle stick into the slit of each foil piece so it reaches to the bottom.
6. Place in the freezer for about 6 hours.
7. Carefully, remove the popsicles from cups and enjoy.

Pitkin
Pops

Prep Time: 20 mins
Total Time: 20 mins

Servings per Recipe: 5
Calories   516.0
Fat   36.8 g
Cholesterol   0.0 mg
Sodium   143.9 mg
Carbohydrates   44.3 g
Protein   11.4 g

Ingredients
5-10 bananas
1 C. almonds, crushed
1 C. walnuts, crushed
1 C. carob powder
1 C. dried coconut

Directions
1. In 4 separate plates, place the almonds, walnuts, carob powder and coconut respectively.
2. Coat each banana with the almonds, followed by the walnuts, carob powder and coconut.
3. Arrange the bananas onto a wax paper lined baking sheet and place in the freezer until chilled.
4. Enjoy.

CUBAN
Paletas

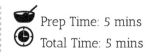
Prep Time: 5 mins
Total Time: 5 mins

Servings per Recipe: 8
Calories	175.6
Fat	6.4 g
Cholesterol	0.0 mg
Sodium	14.5 mg
Carbohydrates	29.8 g
Protein	0.8 g

Ingredients
1 (5 oz.) cans pineapple chunks in light
syrup
1 (10 1/2 oz.) cans coconut milk
2 bananas, peeled
1 tsp. vanilla

Directions
1. In a food processor, add all the ingredients and pulse until smooth.
2. Transfer the mixture into Popsicle molds and place in the freezer for about 3 hours.
3. Carefully, remove the popsicles from molds and enjoy.

Madrona
Paletas

Prep Time: 10 mins
Total Time: 6 h 10 mins

Servings per Recipe: 6
Calories   99.6
Fat   0.4 g
Cholesterol   0.0 mg
Sodium   1.2 mg
Carbohydrates   25.1 g
Protein   0.9 g

Ingredients
2 fresh mangoes, peeled, pitted and diced
1/4-1/2 C. sugar
1 tsp. lemon juice

Directions
1. In a food processor, add all the ingredients and pulse until smooth.
2. Transfer the mixture into Popsicle molds evenly.
3. Now, insert 1 Popsicle stick into each mold and place in the freezer for about 6 hours.
4. Carefully, remove the popsicles from molds and enjoy.

CITY HEIGHTS
Paletas

Prep Time: 20 mins
Total Time: 20 mins

Servings per Recipe: 1
Calories   51.9
Fat   1.7 g
Cholesterol   5.8 mg
Sodium   48.1 mg
Carbohydrates   8.6 g
Protein   0.7 g

Ingredients
2 C. Trix cereal
4 C. vanilla almond milk
2 large scoop vanilla ice cream

Directions
1. In a bowl, add the cereal and milk and keep aside for about 10-15 minutes.
2. In another bowl, add the ice cream and keep aside until liquid.
3. Add the cereal mixture into the bowl of the ice cream and mix until well combined.
4. Transfer the mixture into Popsicle molds and place in the freezer for about 45 minutes.
5. Now, insert 1 Popsicle stick into each mold and place in the freezer for about 4 hours.
6. Carefully, remove the popsicles from molds and enjoy.

Popsicle
of Natural Colours

🥣 Prep Time: 4 h
🕐 Total Time: 4 h

Servings per Recipe: 12
Calories	76.0
Fat	0.9 g
Cholesterol	2.9 mg
Sodium	15.7 mg
Carbohydrates	16.8 g
Protein	1.5 g

Ingredients

Red
1/3 C. frozen strawberries
1/3 C. frozen raspberries
1/2 frozen banana
2 tbsp. yogurt
1/3 C. water

Orange
1/2 C. frozen mango
1/2 frozen banana
1/4 C. orange
1/4 C. yogurt
1/3 water

Green
1 handful spinach
1 frozen banana
1/4 C. yogurt
1/3 C. water

Blue
1 table spoon blue spirulina
1/2 C. frozen pineapple
1 frozen banana
1/4 C. yogurt
1/3 C. water

Magenta
1/3 C. beet
1/2 C. frozen raspberries
1/2 frozen banana
1/4 C. yogurt
1/3 C. water

Directions

1. For red layer in a food processor, add all the ingredients and pulse until smooth.
2. Repeat with the remaining 3 layers ingredients.
3. Place the layers into each Popsicle mold, one layer at a time.
4. Now, insert 1 Popsicle stick into each mold and place in the freezer until set completely.
5. Carefully, remove the popsicles from molds and enjoy.

MY FIRST
Popsicle

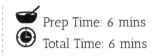 Prep Time: 6 mins

Total Time: 6 mins

Servings per Recipe: 6
Calories	12.6
Fat	0.1 g
Cholesterol	0.0 mg
Sodium	1.0 mg
Carbohydrates	3.1 g
Protein	0.2 g

Ingredients
1 1/2 C. sliced fresh strawberries
1/2-1 C. ice cube
2 tbsp. lemon juice
Water,-1/2 C. to 1 C.
Agave

Directions
1. In a food processor, add all the ingredients and pulse until smooth.
2. Transfer the mixture into Popsicle molds evenly.
3. Now, insert 1 Popsicle stick into each mold and place in the freezer overnight.
4. Carefully, remove the popsicles from molds and enjoy.

2-Ingredient
Paletas

🥣 Prep Time: 20 mins
🕐 Total Time: 20 mins

Servings per Recipe: 10
Calories	30.2
Fat	0.1 g
Cholesterol	0.0 mg
Sodium	0.5 mg
Carbohydrates	7.6 g
Protein	0.4 g

Ingredients

2 ripe bananas, sliced
2 C. fresh strawberries, sliced

Directions

1. In a food processor, add all the ingredients and pulse until smooth.
2. Transfer the mixture into Popsicle molds evenly.
3. Now, insert 1 Popsicle stick into each mold and place in the freezer until set completely.
4. Carefully, remove the popsicles from molds and enjoy.

AMERICAN
Dream Paletas

🥣 Prep Time: 40 mins
🕐 Total Time: 2 h 40 mins

Servings per Recipe: 8
Calories	68.6
Fat	3.0 g
Cholesterol	0.0 mg
Sodium	3.6 mg
Carbohydrates	11.3 g
Protein	0.5 g

Ingredients

1 C. frozen strawberries
1/2 C. water
1 tsp. honey
1/2 C. coconut milk
1 tsp. honey

1 C. frozen blueberries
1/2 C. water
1 tsp. honey

Directions

1. In a food processor, add the strawberries, honey and water and pulse until smooth.
2. Place about 1 tbsp. of the strawberry mixture into each Popsicle mold and place in the freezer for about 40 minutes.
3. In the clean food processor, add the honey and coconut milk and pulse until smooth.
4. Remove the popsicles from freezer and place 1 tbsp. of the honey mixture into each mold.
5. Then, insert 1 Popsicle stick in each mold and place in the freezer for about 40 minutes.
6. In the clean food processor, add the blueberries, honey and water and pulse until smooth.
7. Remove the popsicles from freezer and place about 2 tbsp. of the blueberry mixture into each mold.
8. Place in the freezer for about 1 hour.
9. Carefully, remove the popsicles from molds and enjoy.

Chili
Peanut Pops

Prep Time: 10 mins
Total Time: 10 mins

Servings per Recipe: 1

Calories	2251.6
Fat	142.7 g
Cholesterol	34.1 mg
Sodium	1897.7 mg
Carbohydrates	217.1 g
Protein	78.4 g

Ingredients

1 C. peanut butter
1/2 C. liquid honey
3/4 tsp. cayenne pepper
1/4 tsp. salt
1/3 C. unsweetened cocoa powder
1 C. milk
1 tbsp. peanuts, very finely chopped

Directions

1. In a bowl, add the honey, peanut butter, cocoa powder, cayenne and salt and mix until smooth.
2. Slowly, add the milk and beat until smooth.
3. In the bottom of each Popsicle mold, place the peanuts and top with the milk mixture evenly.
4. Now, insert 1 Popsicle stick into each mold and place in the freezer for about 6 hours.
5. Carefully, remove the popsicles from molds and enjoy.

CREAM CHEESE
Paletas

Prep Time: 4 hr
Total Time: 4 hr

Servings per Recipe: 16

Calories	157.5
Fat	8.3 g
Cholesterol	27.4 mg
Sodium	83.4 mg
Carbohydrates	19.2 g
Protein	2.4 g

Ingredients

10 oz. blueberries
1 1/4 C. water
1 tbsp. lemon juice
1/2 C. sugar
1 tbsp. cornstarch
2 C. plain yogurt
12 oz. cream cheese, softened

1 tbsp. lemon juice
1 C. powdered sugar

Directions

1. In a bowl, dissolve the cornstarch into 1/4 C. of the water.
2. In a pot, add the blueberries, sugar, lemon juice and remaining water and cook until heated completely.
3. Stir in the cornstarch mixture and cook until mixture becomes thick, stirring continuously.
4. Remove from the heat and keep aside to cool.
5. In a bowl, add the cream cheese, yogurt, sugar and lemon juice and with a hand mixer, beat until smooth.
6. Place the blueberry mixture and yogurt mixture into each Popsicle mold in desired layers.
7. Place in the freezer for about 1 hour.
8. Now, insert 1 Popsicle stick into each mold and place in the freezer for about 4 hours.
9. Carefully, remove the popsicles from molds and enjoy.

Cedar Mountain
Popsicles

Prep Time: 15 mins
Total Time: 3 h 15 mins

Servings per Recipe: 1
Calories   82.3
Fat   0.1 g
Cholesterol   0.0 mg
Sodium   0.5 mg
Carbohydrates   21.6 g
Protein   0.8 g

Ingredients

2 C. black cherries, pitted
2 tbsp. lime juice
2 tbsp. honey

Directions

1. In a food processor, add all the ingredients and pulse until smooth.
2. Through a wire mesh sieve, strain the mixture into a bowl.
3. Transfer the mixture into Popsicle molds evenly.
4. Now, insert 1 Popsicle stick into each mold and place in the freezer until set completely.
5. Carefully, remove the popsicles from molds and enjoy.

LATIN LUNCH
Popsicles

Prep Time: 5 mins
Total Time: 5 mins

Servings per Recipe: 4
Calories	25.6
Fat	0.0 g
Cholesterol	0.0 mg
Sodium	1.2 mg
Carbohydrates	6.8 g
Protein	0.1 g

Ingredients
1 C. unsweetened applesauce
1/4-1/3 C. dulce de leche

Directions
1. In the bottom of each Popsicle mold, place the applesauce about 2/3 full.
2. Place some dulce de leche in the center of each mold and with a spoon, push down lightly.
3. Now, fill each mold with the remaining applesauce.
4. Now, insert 1 Popsicle stick into each mold and place in the freezer until set completely.
5. Carefully, remove the popsicles from molds and enjoy.

Spiced
Creamer Pops

🥣 Prep Time: 10 mins
🕐 Total Time: 10 mins

Servings per Recipe: 8
Calories	27.0
Fat	0.1 g
Cholesterol	0.0 mg
Sodium	0.3 mg
Carbohydrates	6.8 g
Protein	0.3 g

Ingredients

2 bananas
1 C. silk soy coffee creamer
1/2 tsp. cinnamon
1/4 tsp. vanilla extract

Directions

1. In a food processor, add all the ingredients and pulse until smooth.
2. Transfer the mixture into Popsicle molds evenly.
3. Now, insert 1 Popsicle stick into each mold and place in the freezer until set completely.
4. Carefully, remove the popsicles from molds and enjoy.

MAKE-AHEAD
Paletas

Prep Time: 5 mins
Total Time: 8 h 5 mins

Servings per Recipe: 4
Calories	64.4
Fat	0.0 g
Cholesterol	0.0 mg
Sodium	0.8 mg
Carbohydrates	17.4 g
Protein	0.0 g

Ingredients
2/3 C. fresh fruit, thawed and pureed
2/3 C. unsweetened fruit juice
1/4-1/3 C. honey
1 tbsp. fruit jell freezer jam pectin
popsicle molds

Directions
1. In a bowl, add the honey, fruit puree and fruit juice and mix until well combined.
2. Add 1 rounded tbsp. of the pectin and mix for about 3 minutes.
3. Transfer the mixture into Popsicle molds evenly.
4. Now, insert 1 Popsicle stick into each mold and place in the freezer for about 10-12 hours.
5. Carefully, remove the popsicles from molds and enjoy.

Healthy
Coco Pops

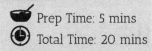

Prep Time: 5 mins
Total Time: 20 mins

Servings per Recipe: 4
Calories	104.3
Fat	4.5 g
Cholesterol	17.0 mg
Sodium	60.0 mg
Carbohydrates	12.4 g
Protein	4.3 g

Ingredients
1 (1 1/3 oz.) boxes instant chocolate
pudding mix
2 C. milk
1 banana

Directions
1. Prepare the pudding according to package's directions.
2. Transfer the mixture into Popsicle molds alongside banana pieces in each one.
3. Now, insert 1 Popsicle stick into each mold and place in the freezer until set completely.
4. Carefully, remove the popsicles from molds and enjoy.

HAWAIIAN
Paletas

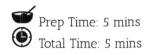
Prep Time: 5 mins
Total Time: 5 mins

Servings per Recipe: 8

Calories	76.7
Fat	1.0 g
Cholesterol	3.7 mg
Sodium	14.2 mg
Carbohydrates	15.9 g
Protein	1.7 g

Ingredients
1 (8 oz.) cartons vanilla yogurt
1 (8 oz.) cans crushed pineapple, undrained
6 oz. frozen pineapple orange juice
concentrate, thawed
8 paper, drink C.
8 wooden sticks

Directions
1. In a food processor, add the pineapple, yogurt and juice concentrate and pulse until smooth.
2. Transfer the mixture into the paper cups evenly.
3. Place in the freezer for about 1 hour.
4. Now, insert 1 Popsicle stick into each cup and place in the freezer for about 2 hours.
5. Carefully, remove the popsicles from cups and enjoy.

Pennsylvania
Paletas

Prep Time: 5 mins

Total Time: 3 h 5 mins

Servings per Recipe: 8
Calories	60.0
Fat	1.1 g
Cholesterol	4.2 mg
Sodium	15.7 mg
Carbohydrates	11.8 g
Protein	1.1 g

Ingredients
1 C. milk
3/4 C. grape juice
1/4 C. sugar
1/4 C. lemon juice

Directions
1. In a bowl, add all the ingredients and beat until well combined and cover with the lids tightly.
2. Transfer the mixture into 8 Tupperware Popsicle molds.
3. Cover each mold with the lid tightly and place in the freezer until set completely.
4. Carefully, remove the popsicles from molds and enjoy.

AUSTRALIAN
Hazelnut Pops

 Prep Time: 10 mins
Total Time: 10 mins

Servings per Recipe: 6
Calories	170.6
Fat	9.3 g
Cholesterol	6.1 mg
Sodium	36.3 mg
Carbohydrates	18.2 g
Protein	3.2 g

Ingredients
1/2 C. nutella
1 1/2 C. whole milk
popsicle molds
Dixie paper C.
popsicle stick

Directions
1. In a bowl, add the milk and Nutella and mix until well combined.
2. Transfer the mixture into Popsicle molds and place in the freezer until set completely.
3. Carefully, remove the popsicles from molds and enjoy.

Flavors
of October Pops

Prep Time: 5 mins
Total Time: 11 mins

Servings per Recipe: 1
Calories	124.7
Fat	3.2 g
Cholesterol	10.5 mg
Sodium	12.4 mg
Carbohydrates	24.7 g
Protein	1.5 g

Ingredients
2 1/2 lb. butternut squash
1/2 C. maple syrup

2/3 C. light cream
1/2-3/4 tsp. pumpkin pie spice

Directions
1. In a pan of the water, add the butternut squash and cook until cooked through.
2. Drain the squash well and transfer into a bowl.
3. With a potato masher, mash the squash until creamy.
4. Add the remaining ingredients and mix until well combined.
5. Transfer the mixture into Popsicle molds evenly.
6. Now, insert 1 Popsicle stick into each mold and place in the freezer for about 6 hours.
7. Carefully, remove the popsicles from molds and enjoy.

YELLOW STONE
Paletas

 Prep Time: 10 mins

Total Time: 4 h 10 mins

Servings per Recipe: 1

Calories	223.6
Fat	8.9 g
Cholesterol	34.1 mg
Sodium	120.1 mg
Carbohydrates	24.7 g
Protein	8.0 g

Ingredients
2 C. milk
2 tbsp. sugar
1 tbsp. vanilla
1 small paper C.
wooden popsicle sticks

Directions
1. In a bowl, add the sugar, milk and vanilla and mix until well combined.
2. Transfer the mixture into the paper cups about half way full.
3. Place in the freezer for about 1 hour.
4. Now, insert 1 Popsicle stick into each cup and place in the freezer for about 4 hours.
5. Carefully, remove the popsicles from cups and enjoy.

Alabama Porch
Paletas

Prep Time: 15 mins
Total Time: 15 mins

Servings per Recipe: 6
Calories   72.7
Fat   0.1 g
Cholesterol   0.0 mg
Sodium   48.5 mg
Carbohydrates   18.2 g
Protein   0.6 g

Ingredients
3 medium peaches, pitted and 1/4-inch pieces
1/2 C. soy yogurt
1/3 C. sugar

1/3 C. vanilla unsweetened almond milk
1/4 tsp. almond extract
1/8 tsp. fine salt

Directions
1. In a bowl, reserve about 1 C. of the peach pieces.
2. In a food processor, add the remaining peach pieces and all other ingredients and pulse until smooth.
3. Transfer the mixture into Popsicle molds evenly.
4. Now, insert 1 Popsicle stick into each mold and place in the freezer until set completely.
5. Carefully, remove the popsicles from molds and enjoy.

MEDITERRANEAN
Agave Pops

Prep Time: 10 mins
Total Time: 10 mins

Servings per Recipe: 8
Calories	26.5
Fat	0.0 g
Cholesterol	0.0 mg
Sodium	0.0 mg
Carbohydrates	6.2 g
Protein	0.4 g

Ingredients
2 C. fresh pitted cherries
2 C. plain unsweteened kefir
2 tbsp. Agave
1 1/2-2 tsp. almond extract

Directions
1. In a food processor, add all the ingredients and pulse until smooth.
2. Transfer the mixture into 8 (3-oz.) Popsicle molds evenly.
3. Now, insert 1 Popsicle stick into each mold and place in the freezer for about 3 hours.
4. Carefully, remove the popsicles from molds and enjoy.

Lemon Maraschino
Paletas

Prep Time: 10 mins
Total Time: 10 mins

Servings per Recipe: 4
Calories   108.7
Fat   0.1 g
Cholesterol   0.0 mg
Sodium   7.3 mg
Carbohydrates   27.2 g
Protein   0.4 g

Ingredients

2 C. diet lemon-lime soda
1/2 C. orange juice
1 (8 oz.) jars maraschino cherries

Directions

1. In a bowl, add the orange juice and soda and mix until well combined.
2. Transfer the mixture into Popsicle molds alongside 2-4 cherries into each.
3. Transfer the mixture into Popsicle molds evenly.
4. Now, insert 1 Popsicle stick into each mold and place in the freezer until firm completely.
5. Carefully, remove the popsicles from molds and enjoy.

WILD BERRY
Pops

Prep Time: 10 mins
Total Time: 10 h 10 mins

Servings per Recipe: 6
Calories	59.7
Fat	0.2 g
Cholesterol	0.0 mg
Sodium	0.9 mg
Carbohydrates	15.1 g
Protein	0.6 g

Ingredients
2 tbsp. lime juice
3 tbsp. organic sugar
1 1/4 C. thawed unsweetened strawberries
1 C. frozen unsweetened pineapple chunks
1 C. frozen unsweetened raspberries

Directions
1. In a food processor, add all the ingredients in batches and pulse until smooth.
2. Transfer the mixture into 5 paper cups evenly.
3. Now, insert 1 Popsicle stick into each cup.
4. Place in the freezer overnight.
5. Carefully, remove the popsicles from cups and enjoy.

2-Ingredient
Coffee Paletas

Prep Time: 5 mins
Total Time: 10 mins

Servings per Recipe: 6
Calories   110.7
Fat   2.9 g
Cholesterol   11.5 mg
Sodium   43.9 mg
Carbohydrates   18.8 g
Protein   2.7 g

Ingredients

2 C. extra-strong coffee
2/3 C. sweetened condensed milk

Directions

1. In a bowl, add the condensed milk and coffee and mix until well combined.
2. Transfer the mixture into Popsicle molds evenly.
3. Now, insert 1 Popsicle stick into each mold and place in the freezer until set completely.
4. Carefully, remove the popsicles from molds and enjoy.

MS. WONG'S
Popsicles

Prep Time: 20 mins
Total Time: 6 h 20 mins

Servings per Recipe: 12
Calories	115.9
Fat	11.6 g
Cholesterol	0.0 mg
Sodium	16.3 mg
Carbohydrates	3.6 g
Protein	1.1 g

Ingredients
1/2 C. fresh avocado
2 1/3 C. unsweetened almond coconut milk
18 drops stevia
1/2 C. shredded sweetened flaked coconut

Directions
1. In a food processor, add all the ingredients and pulse until smooth.
2. Transfer the mixture into Popsicle molds evenly.
3. Now, insert 1 Popsicle stick into each mold and place in the freezer until set completely.
4. Carefully, remove the popsicles from molds and enjoy.

New Zealand
Pops

Prep Time: 5 mins
Total Time: 2 h 5 mins

Servings per Recipe: 6
Calories   18.7
Fat   0.1 g
Cholesterol   0.0 mg
Sodium   1.6 mg
Carbohydrates   4.4 g
Protein   0.2 g

Ingredients

1 small kiwi fruit, peeled and diced
1/3 C. small raspberries
1-1 1/4 C. light cranberry juice

Directions

1. In the bottom of 6 (2-oz.) Popsicle molds place the raspberries and kiwi pieces evenly and top with the cranberry juice.
2. Now, insert 1 Popsicle stick into each mold and place in the freezer for about 2 hours.
3. Carefully, remove the popsicles from mods and enjoy.

PROTEIN POWER
Paletas

Prep Time: 3 hr
Total Time: 3 hr 3 mins

Servings per Recipe: 6
Calories	112.5
Fat	5.8 g
Cholesterol	2.0 mg
Sodium	67.6 mg
Carbohydrates	12.4 g
Protein	4.0 g

Ingredients
1/2 C. water
1/4 C. sugar
1/4 C. peanut butter
1 C. low-fat milk

Directions
1. In a pan, add the sugar and water and cook until boiling.
2. Cook for about 3 minutes, stirring frequently.
3. Remove from the heat and stir in the peanut butter until well combined.
4. Add the milk and mix until well combined.
5. Keep aside to cool for about 12-15 minutes.
6. Transfer the mixture into 6 (5-oz.) paper cups evenly.
7. Now, insert 1 Popsicle stick into each cup.
8. Place in the freezer until set completely.
9. Remove the cups from the freezer and keep aside at room temperature for about 3 minutes.
10. Carefully, remove the popsicles from cups and enjoy.

Canadian
Grapefruit Pops

Prep Time: 3 hr
Total Time: 3 hr 30 mins

Servings per Recipe: 1
Calories	62.6
Fat	0.1 g
Cholesterol	0.0 mg
Sodium	2.4 mg
Carbohydrates	15.7 g
Protein	0.4 g

Ingredients
3/4 C. grapefruit juice, freshly squeezed
3/4 C. orange juice, freshly squeezed
1/4 C. lime juice, freshly squeezed
1/4 C. maple syrup

Directions
1. Through a wire mesh sieve, strain each fresh fruit juice into a bowl, discarding any pulp and seeds.
2. Add the maple syrup and beat until well combined.
3. Transfer the mixture into Popsicle molds evenly.
4. Now, insert 1 Popsicle stick into each mold and place in the freezer for about 3-5 hours.
5. Carefully, remove the popsicles from molds and enjoy.

LIMON GRAND
Mundo Paletas

Prep Time: 20 min
Total Time: 4 hr 20 mins

Servings per Recipe: 10
Calories   92.1
Fat   1.4 g
Cholesterol   5.1 mg
Sodium   34.7 mg
Carbohydrates   17.9 g
Protein   2.8 g

Ingredients
Lemon
1 1/3 C. low-fat yogurt, plain
1/4 C. fresh lemon juice
5 tbsp. sugar
Berry
1 pint strawberry, cored and quartered
1/4 C. sugar

2 tbsp. water
1 tsp. lemon juice
1 C. plain yogurt

Directions
1. For the lemonade layer: in a microwave-safe bowl, add the lemon juice and sugar and microwave for about 45 seconds.
2. In another bowl, add the yogurt and sugar mixture and beat until smooth.
3. Place in the fridge until using.
4. For the strawberry layer: mixture: in a pot, add the strawberries, sugar and water and cook until boiling.
5. Cook for about 5 minutes, mixing occasionally.
6. In a blender, add the strawberry mixture and lemon juice and process until just pureed. But not liquefied.
7. Place in the fridge to cool.
8. Add the yogurt and beat until blended nicely.
9. Place about 1 tbsp. of the each lemon and strawberry mixture into Popsicle molds in layers.
10. Now, insert 1 Popsicle stick into each mold and place in the freezer overnight.
11. Carefully, remove the popsicles from molds and enjoy.

Bonnie's
Best Pops

Prep Time: 3 hr
Total Time: 6 hr 30 mins

Servings per Recipe: 20
Calories	84.2
Fat	0.3 g
Cholesterol	0.0 mg
Sodium	2.2 mg
Carbohydrates	21.2 g
Protein	1.6 g

Ingredients

1 seedless watermelon, small, peeled and chunks
2 red grapefruits, sweet ruby red
preferred, juiced
2 oranges, large, juiced

Directions

1. In a food processor, add the watermelon and pulse until pureed.
2. Through a sieve, strain the watermelon puree into a bowl.
3. Through the sieve, strain the grapefruit and oranges juice into the bowl of the watermelon juice and mix well.
4. Transfer the mixture into Popsicle molds evenly.
5. Now, insert 1 Popsicle stick into each mold and place in the freezer for about 6 hours.
6. Carefully, remove the popsicles from molds and enjoy.

BROOKLYN
Bridge Pops

Prep Time: 15 min
Total Time: 2 hr 45 mins

Servings per Recipe: 10

Calories	71.7
Fat	0.5 g
Cholesterol	0.6 mg
Sodium	39.5 mg
Carbohydrates	15.4 g
Protein	1.7 g

Ingredients

8 oz. mascarpone cheese
1/4 C. fat free Greek yogurt
1 C. skim milk
3 tbsp. sugar

1/2 C. graham cracker, crushed
1 C. frozen raspberries
1 tsp. lemon juice

Directions

1. In a bowl, add the milk, yogurt, mascarpone and 2 tbsp. of the sugar and beat until smooth and creamy.

2. Gently fold in the graham crackers. Set

3. In a food processor, add the raspberries, remaining sugar and lemon juice and pulse until blended finely.

4. Add the raspberry mixture into the cheesecake mixture and gently, stir to combine.

5. Transfer the mixture into Popsicle molds evenly and place in the freezer for about 30 minutes.

6. Now, insert 1 Popsicle stick into each mold and place in the freezer for about 3 hours.

7. Carefully, remove the popsicles from molds and enjoy.

Paletas
Calabasas

Prep Time: 4 hr
Total Time: 5 hr

Servings per Recipe: 8
Calories	213.6
Fat	12.6 g
Cholesterol	42.7 mg
Sodium	107.1 mg
Carbohydrates	24.0 g
Protein	1.9 g

Ingredients

3/4 C. heavy whipping cream
3/4 C. dark brown sugar, packed
2 tbsp. unsalted butter, at room temperature

3/4 tsp. vanilla extract
1/4 tsp. kosher salt
1 tbsp. cornstarch
1 1/2 C. whole milk

Directions

1. In a heavy-based pan, add the cream, butter and brown sugar over medium-high heat and cook until boiling.
2. Set the heat to low and cook for about 10 minutes, mixing often.
3. Add the cornstarch and stir to combine.
4. Gradually, add the milk, beating continuously until smooth.
5. Set the heat to medium and cook for about 5-10 minutes, mixing frequently.
6. Remove from the heat and stir in the vanilla and salt.
7. Keep aside until lukewarm.
8. Transfer the mixture into Popsicle molds evenly.
9. Now, insert 1 Popsicle stick into each mold and place in the freezer overnight.
10. Carefully, remove the popsicles from molds and enjoy.

BASIL
Brasilero Popsicles

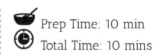 Prep Time: 10 min

Total Time: 10 mins

Servings per Recipe: 1
Calories	52.1
Fat	0.1 g
Cholesterol	0.0 mg
Sodium	49.5 mg
Carbohydrates	13.0 g
Protein	0.4 g

Ingredients
1 pint strawberry, hulled
4 tbsp. sugar
6 large basil leaves
1/4 C. water
1/8 tsp. salt

Directions
1. Cut 3-4 strawberries into slices and keep aside.
2. In a food processor, add the remaining strawberries, basil, sugar, salt and water and pulse until smooth.
3. In the Popsicle molds, divide the strawberry slices evenly.
4. Transfer the mixture into Popsicle molds evenly.
5. Now, insert 1 Popsicle stick into each mold and place in the freezer until set completely.
6. Carefully, remove the popsicles from molds and enjoy.

Juan Pablo
Duarte Pops

🥣 Prep Time: 10 min
🕐 Total Time: 10 min

Servings per Recipe: 1
Calories   50.2
Fat   0.1 g
Cholesterol   0.0 mg
Sodium   99.2 mg
Carbohydrates   12.9 g
Protein   0.7 g

Ingredients

2 large cucumbers peeled and chopped
1/4 C. lime juice
1/4-1/2 jalapeño, finely chopped seeds removed

4 tbsp. sugar
1/4 tsp. salt
zest of two lime

Directions

1. In a food processor, add the cucumbers, jalapeño, sugar, salt and lime juice and process until smooth.
2. Transfer the mixture into a bowl and gently, stir in the reserved cucumbers and lime zest.
3. Now, transfer the mixture into Popsicle molds evenly.
4. Now, insert 1 Popsicle stick into each mold and place in the freezer until set completely.
5. Carefully, remove the popsicles from molds and enjoy.

KIWI
Cream Pops

Prep Time: 10 min
Total Time: 10 mins

Servings per Recipe: 10
Calories	44.9
Fat	0.9 g
Cholesterol	3.1 mg
Sodium	13.2 mg
Carbohydrates	8.3 g
Protein	1.2 g

Ingredients
2 kiwi fruits, peeled and 15-20 small
chunks
1 C. organic concord grape juice
1 C. plain yogurt, with fat
2 tsp. vanilla syrup
1 C. raspberries
1/4-1/2 C. water

Directions
1. In the Popsicle molds, divide half of the kiwi chunks evenly.
2. In a bowl, add the grape juice, half of the yogurt and half of the vanilla and beat until smooth.
3. Transfer the yogurt mixture into Popsicle molds, about half way through.
4. Freeze for about 10 minutes.
5. In a food processor, add the raspberries, 1/4 C. of the water and remaining vanilla and beat until smooth.
6. Remove the molds from the freezer.
7. Now, divide the remaining kiwi chunks into the molds.
8. Transfer the raspberry mixture into Popsicle molds evenly.
9. Now, insert 1 Popsicle stick into each mold and place in the freezer for about 6 hours.
10. Carefully, remove the popsicles from molds and enjoy.

Ruby's
Country Paletas

Prep Time: 5 min
Total Time: 10 min

Servings per Recipe: 4
Calories	226.6
Fat	2.5 g
Cholesterol	7.9 mg
Sodium	34.1 mg
Carbohydrates	50.0 g
Protein	3.9 g

Ingredients
1 lb. rhubarb
2/3 C. sugar
1 lb. strawberry
1 C. plain yogurt

Directions
1. In a pot, add the sugar and rhubarb over medium heat and cook until rhubarb is done completely, mixing often.
2. Remove from the heat and transfer the rhubarb mixture in a food processor alongside the strawberries and yogurt and pulse until smooth.
3. Transfer the mixture into Popsicle molds evenly.
4. Now, insert 1 Popsicle stick into each mold and place in the freezer until set completely.
5. Carefully, remove the popsicles from molds and enjoy.

BAJA
Paletas

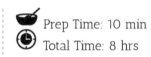 Prep Time: 10 min

Total Time: 8 hrs

Servings per Recipe: 10	
Calories	48.8
Fat	0.1 g
Cholesterol	0.0 mg
Sodium	13.2 mg
Carbohydrates	12.7 g
Protein	0.4 g

Ingredients
1/4 C. sugar, super fine
1/4 C. water
4 C. honeydew melon, peeled, seeded and
cut
2/3 C. fresh lime juice

Directions
1. In a pot, add the sugar and water and cook until sugar is dissolved, stirring continuously.
2. In a food processor, add half of the melon and half of lime juice and pulse until smooth.
3. Add the remaining melon, sugar syrup and remaining lime juice and pulse until smooth.
4. Through a fine mesh sieve, strain the mixture into a bowl, pressing the solids with the back of a spoon.
5. Transfer the mixture into Popsicle molds evenly and place in the freezer for about 2 hours.
6. Now, insert 1 Popsicle stick into each mold and place in the freezer for about 6 hours.
7. Carefully, remove the popsicles from molds and enjoy.

Electrolyte Paletas

🥣 Prep Time: 1 hr
🕐 Total Time: 1 hr

Servings per Recipe: 1
Calories	0.0
Fat	0.0 g
Cholesterol	0.0 mg
Sodium	4.7 mg
Carbohydrates	0.0 g
Protein	0.0 g

Ingredients

2 tbsp. Gatorade lemon lime powder drink mix
1 wooden stick
1 C. water

Directions

1. In a cup, place the Gatorade powder and water and mix well.
2. Now, insert 1 Popsicle stick into the cup and place in the freezer for about 1 hour.
3. Carefully, remove the Popsicle from cup and enjoy.

CALIFORNIA X FLORIDA
Popsicles

Prep Time: 10 min
Total Time: 2 hr 10 min

Servings per Recipe: 6

Calories	103
Fat	6.7g
Cholesterol	0mg
Sodium	77mg
Carbohydrates	11.3g
Protein	0.8g

Ingredients
1 avocado, peeled and pitted
1/2 C. coconut milk
1/4 C. agave nectar
1/4 C. lime juice
2 tsp. vanilla extract
1/4 tsp. salt

Directions
1. In a food processor, add all the ingredients and pulse until smooth.
2. Transfer the mixture into Popsicle molds evenly.
3. Now, insert 1 Popsicle stick into each mold and place in the freezer for about 2-3 hours.
4. Carefully, remove the popsicles from molds and enjoy.

Minty
Picnic Pops

🥣 Prep Time: 10 mins
🕐 Total Time: 15 mins

Servings per Recipe: 12
Calories   59.8
Fat   0.2 g
Cholesterol   0.0 mg
Sodium   10.7 mg
Carbohydrates   15.5 g
Protein   0.7 g

Ingredients

1/2 honeydew melon, peeled, seeded and 1-inch cubes
2 pints blueberries
1 lime

1/2 C. water
2 tbsp. honey
1 tbsp. finely chopped of fresh mint

Directions

1. In a pot, add the honey, mint, lime zest and water over high heat and cook until boiling.
2. Remove from the heat and keep aside to cool completely.
3. In a food processor, add the blueberries, honeydew and lime juice and pulse until smooth.
4. Through a fine mesh strainer, strain the honey mixture into the food processor with the fruit puree and pulse until well combined.
5. Transfer the mixture into Popsicle molds evenly.
6. Now, insert 1 Popsicle stick into each mold and place in the freezer until set completely.
7. Carefully, remove the popsicles from molds and enjoy.

HOW TO MAKE
Paletas

Prep Time: 10 min
Total Time: 10 min

Servings per Recipe: 6
Calories	66.0
Fat	0.6 g
Cholesterol	2.1 mg
Sodium	5.4 mg
Carbohydrates	14.6 g
Protein	1.0 g

Ingredients
1 (6 oz.) cans frozen orange juice concentrate, softened
1 (6 oz.) cans water
1-8 oz. vanilla ice cream, softened

Directions
1. In a food processor, add all the ingredients and pulse until smooth.
2. Transfer the mixture into Popsicle molds evenly.
3. Now, insert 1 Popsicle stick into each mold and place in the freezer until set completely.
4. Carefully, remove the popsicles from molds and enjoy.

Sweet
Georgian Pops

Prep Time: 20 mins

Total Time: 3 hr 20 mins

Servings per Recipe: 10
Calories	49.2
Fat	0.1 g
Cholesterol	0.0 mg
Sodium	14.9 mg
Carbohydrates	12.8 g
Protein	0.5 g

Ingredients
4 yellow peaches, ripe
2 white peaches, ripe
2 chamomile tea bags
1/4 C. honey
1/2 small lemon, juice of
1 pinch kosher salt

Directions
1. Remove the pit from 2/3 of the peaches.
2. In a food processor, add 2/3 of the peaches with the skins and pulse until just smooth.
3. Transfer the pureed peaches into a bowl.
4. Add the honey, 2 tbsp. of the tea leaves, lemon juice and salt and mix until well combined.
5. Chop the remaining peaches roughly.
6. Add the chopped peaches into the pureed mixture and stir to combine.
7. Transfer the mixture into Popsicle molds evenly.
8. Now, insert 1 Popsicle stick into each mold and place in the freezer until set completely.
9. Carefully, remove the popsicles from molds and enjoy.

COLLEGE QUAD
Popsicles

Prep Time: 5 min
Total Time: 8 hr 5 mins

Servings per Recipe: 4
Calories	103.7
Fat	0.5 g
Cholesterol	1.8 mg
Sodium	26.8 mg
Carbohydrates	22.9 g
Protein	2.1 g

Ingredients
1/4 C. orange juice
3/4 C. low-fat plain yogurt
1/4 C. white sugar
1/2 tsp. vanilla

Directions
1. Divide the orange juice into each Popsicle mold about 1/4 of the full.
2. Freeze for about 2 hours.
3. In a bowl, add the sugar, yogurt and vanilla extract and mix well.
4. Remove the molds from the freezer and fill each with the yogurt mixture.
5. Now, insert 1 Popsicle stick into each mold and place in the freezer overnight.
6. Carefully, remove the popsicles from molds and enjoy.

Lake Fog
Pops

🥣 Prep Time: 10 mins
🕐 Total Time: 10 mins

Servings per Recipe: 6
Calories   55.1
Fat   2.6 g
Cholesterol   10.6 mg
Sodium   40.2 mg
Carbohydrates   5.1 g
Protein   2.9 g

Ingredients

2 C. yogurt, plain low fat
1/2 C. honeydew melon, pureed in
blender

Directions

1. In the bottom of the Popsicle molds, divide the melon puree and yogurt in layers.

2. Now, insert 1 Popsicle stick into each mold and place in the freezer for about hours.

3. Carefully, remove the popsicles from molds and enjoy.

RARE
Popsicles

Prep Time: 10 min
Total Time: 10 mins

Servings per Recipe: 6
Calories	77.1
Fat	0.1 g
Cholesterol	0.0 mg
Sodium	0.7 mg
Carbohydrates	19.5 g
Protein	0.5 g

Ingredients

1 (1 oz.) box sugar-free white chocolate pudding mix, prepared according to package instructions
1 1/2 C. frozen raspberries
1 tbsp. sugar
1/4 C. orange juice

Directions

1. In a food processor, add all the ingredients and pulse until smooth.

2. Transfer the mixture into Popsicle molds evenly.

3. Now, insert 1 Popsicle stick into each mold and place in the freezer for about 4 hours.

4. Carefully, remove the popsicles from molds and enjoy.

Tampa
Pops

Prep Time: 15 mins
Total Time: 4 hr 15 mins

Servings per Recipe: 6
Calories	109.8
Fat	0.2 g
Cholesterol	0.6 mg
Sodium	27.1 mg
Carbohydrates	25.1 g
Protein	3.1 g

Ingredients

7 oz. fat free Greek yogurt
2/3 C. orange juice concentrate, thawed
2 large bananas
1 tbsp. fresh lime juice
1 lime zest

Directions

1. In a food processor, add all the ingredients and pulse until smooth.
2. Transfer the mixture into Popsicle molds evenly.
3. Now, insert 1 Popsicle stick into each mold and place in the freezer for about 4 hours.
4. Carefully, remove the popsicles from molds and enjoy.

PACIFIC
Paletas

Prep Time: 15 min
Total Time: 20 mins

Servings per Recipe: 1
Calories	34.1
Fat	0.0 g
Cholesterol	0.0 mg
Sodium	0.7 mg
Carbohydrates	8.8 g
Protein	0.1 g

Ingredients

1 C. mango puree
1 C. ripe peach puree
1/4 C. water
2 tbsp. sugar
lime juice
6-8 popsicle sticks

Directions

1. In a food processor, add the mango and banana and pulse until smooth.
2. Transfer the pureed fruit into a bowl.
3. In a pan, add the sugar and water and cook until sugar is dissolved, mixing continuously.
4. Transfer the sugar mixture into the bowl of the pureed fruit alongside the lime juice and mix well.
5. Transfer the mixture into Popsicle molds evenly.
6. Now, insert 1 Popsicle stick into each mold and place in the freezer for about 4 hours.
7. Carefully, remove the popsicles from molds and enjoy.

Country Girl
Berry Popsicles

🥣 Prep Time: 5 mins
🕐 Total Time: 5 mins

Servings per Recipe: 10
Calories	77.4
Fat	1.3 g
Cholesterol	4.7 mg
Sodium	17.4 mg
Carbohydrates	15.8 g
Protein	1.7 g

Ingredients

3-4 ripe bananas
1 1/2 C. yogurt
3 tbsp. sugar
1/2 lemon, juice of
1 C. fresh blueberries

Directions

1. In a food processor, add all the ingredients except the blueberries and pulse until smooth.
2. Transfer half of the yogurt mixture into a bowl and keep aside.
3. In the food processor, add the blueberries and process until just blended.
4. Transfer the blueberry mixture into the bowl of the reserved yogurt mixture and with a wooden skewer, swirl slightly.
5. Transfer the mixture into Popsicle molds evenly.
6. Now, insert 1 Popsicle stick into each mold and place in the freezer for about 8 hours.
7. Carefully, remove the popsicles from molds and enjoy.

KAREN'S
Creamy Pops

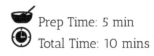 Prep Time: 5 min
Total Time: 10 mins

Servings per Recipe: 4
Calories   128.1
Fat   6.9 g
Cholesterol   22.3 mg
Sodium   26.1 mg
Carbohydrates   15.2 g
Protein   1.8 g

Ingredients
1 C. water
1/4 C. sugar
1 tsp. instant coffee
1 C. half-and-half

Directions
1. In a pan, add 1/4 C. of the sugar, 1 tsp. of the instant coffee and 1 C. of the water and cook for about 3 minutes, mixing continuously.
2. Remove from the heat and stir in 1 C. of the half-and-half.
3. Keep aside to cool.
4. Transfer the mixture into Popsicle molds evenly.
5. Now, insert 1 Popsicle stick into each mold and place in the freezer until set completely.
6. Carefully, remove the popsicles from molds and enjoy.

3-Ingredient
Paletas

🥣 Prep Time: 10 mins
🕐 Total Time: 10 mins

Servings per Recipe: 10
Calories   49.3
Fat   0.1 g
Cholesterol   0.0 mg
Sodium   2.5 mg
Carbohydrates   12.4 g
Protein   0.4 g

Ingredients
4 kiwi fruits, peeled
1 (6 oz.) cans lemonade concentrate
2 C. water

Directions
1. In a food processor, add the kiwi and pulse until just smooth.
2. Transfer the pureed kiwi into a bowl and stir in the lemonade concentrate and water.
3. Transfer the mixture into Popsicle molds evenly and place in the freezer until set partially.
4. Now, insert 1 Popsicle stick into each mold and place in the freezer until set completely.
5. Carefully, remove the popsicles from molds and enjoy.

MANGO
Toscana Pops

Prep Time: 10 min
Total Time: 6 hr 10 mins

Servings per Recipe: 6
Calories   46.2
Fat   0.1 g
Cholesterol   0.0 mg
Sodium   3.9 mg
Carbohydrates   11.9 g
Protein   0.3 g

Ingredients

1 ripe mango
1/2 C. loosely packed chopped parsley
1/4 C. organic frozen lemonade concentrate

Directions

1. In a food processor, add all the ingredients and pulse until smooth.
2. Transfer the mixture into Popsicle molds evenly.
3. Now, insert 1 Popsicle stick into each mold and place in the freezer for about 6 hours.
4. Carefully, remove the popsicles from molds and enjoy.

After-School Paletas

🥣 Prep Time: 10 mins
🕐 Total Time: 6 hr 10 mins

Servings per Recipe: 6
Calories   79.8
Fat   0.1 g
Cholesterol   0.0 mg
Sodium   1.4 mg
Carbohydrates   20.7 g
Protein   0.6 g

Ingredients
3 C. pineapple chunks
1/2 tsp. cinnamon
1/4 C. fresh orange juice

Directions
1. In a food processor, add all the ingredients and pulse until smooth.
2. Transfer the mixture into Popsicle molds evenly.
3. Now, insert 1 Popsicle stick into each mold and place in the freezer for about 6 hours.
4. Carefully, remove the popsicles from molds and enjoy.

LEMON PESTO
Paletas

Prep Time: 10 min
Total Time: 6 hr 10 mins

Servings per Recipe: 6
Calories	87.0
Fat	0.2 g
Cholesterol	0.0 mg
Sodium	48.1 mg
Carbohydrates	22.2 g
Protein	0.7 g

Ingredients
4 C. cubed honeydew melon
1/4 C. chopped fresh basil
1/2 C. organic frozen lemonade concentrate
1 dash salt

Directions
1. In a food processor, add all the ingredients and pulse until smooth.
2. Transfer the mixture into Popsicle molds evenly.
3. Now, insert 1 Popsicle stick into each mold and place in the freezer for about 6 hours.
4. Carefully, remove the popsicles from molds and enjoy.

Berry
Blast Pops

🥣 Prep Time: 10 mins
🕐 Total Time: 10 mins

Servings per Recipe: 1
Calories   100.2
Fat   0.5 g
Cholesterol   0.0 mg
Sodium   1.3 mg
Carbohydrates   24.7 g
Protein   1.1 g

Ingredients

7 oz. strawberries, halved
7 oz. raspberries
4 oz. watermelon, deseeded, cubed
4 tbsp. superfine sugar

Directions

1. In a food processor, add all the ingredients and pulse until smooth.
2. Transfer the mixture into Popsicle molds evenly.
3. Now, insert 1 Popsicle stick into each mold and place in the freezer until set completely.
4. Carefully, remove the popsicles from molds and enjoy.

MARIA'S
Vanilla Pops

Prep Time: 5 min
Total Time: 4 hr 5 mins

Servings per Recipe: 12

Calories	40.6
Fat	0.1 g
Cholesterol	0.0 mg
Sodium	51.0 mg
Carbohydrates	9.7 g
Protein	0.7 g

Ingredients
4 C. strawberries, hulled
1 C. non-fat vanilla yogurt
1/2 C. fat-free sweetened condensed milk
3 C. corn flakes, crushed

Directions
1. In a food processor, add the strawberries and pulse until pureed.
2. Transfer the pureed strawberries into a bowl with the yogurt and milk and mix well.
3. Transfer the mixture into Popsicle molds evenly.
4. Now, insert 1 Popsicle stick into each mold and place in the freezer for about 4 hours.
5. Carefully, remove the popsicles from molds and coat each with the cereal.
6. Enjoy.

Sanibel
Island Pops

Prep Time: 30 mins
Total Time: 35 mins

Servings per Recipe: 8
Calories	227.5
Fat	13.0 g
Cholesterol	42.6 mg
Sodium	126.0 mg
Carbohydrates	27.0 g
Protein	2.5 g

Ingredients

8 oz. cream cheese, softened
1/4 C. honey
2 C. frozen berries, thawed and drained
(raspberries)

2/3 C. juice, from berries and water to yield
3 C. miniature marshmallows, optional
2 C. whipped cream

Directions

1. In a bowl, add the cream cheese and with an electric mixer, beat until smooth.
2. Slowly, add the honey and beat on low speed until well combined.
3. Add the raspberries and the reserved juice mixture and mix well.
4. Add the whipped cream and marshmallows and gently, stir to combine.
5. Place about 1/2 C. of the mixture into each paper cup
6. Now, insert 1 Popsicle stick into each cup and place in the freezer for about 4 hours.
7. Carefully, remove the popsicles from cups and enjoy.

SPANISH
Cucumber Paletas

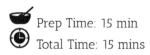

Prep Time: 15 min
Total Time: 15 mins

Servings per Recipe: 4
Calories	46.4
Fat	0.1 g
Cholesterol	0.0 mg
Sodium	2.5 mg
Carbohydrates	11.6 g
Protein	0.8 g

Ingredients
1 large cucumber, grated
1/2 C. fresh pineapple chunk
1/2 C. pineapple juice
1 tbsp. simple syrup
1/2 C. fresh pineapple, diced and frozen

Directions
1. Place the grated cucumber into a cheesecloth-lined strainer and squeeze the cheesecloth to extract the liquid into a bowl.
2. In a food processor, add the pineapple chunks with the juice, 1/2 C. of the cucumber water and sugar syrup and pulse until pureed.
3. Transfer the mixture into Popsicle molds alongside the diced pineapple evenly.
4. Now, insert 1 Popsicle stick into each mold and place in the freezer until set completely.
5. Carefully, remove the popsicles from molds and enjoy.

Spicy
Mexicana Paletas

🥣 Prep Time: 15 mins
🕐 Total Time: 15 mins

Servings per Recipe: 6

Calories	73.0
Fat	0.3 g
Cholesterol	0.0 mg
Sodium	27.9 mg
Carbohydrates	18.4 g
Protein	0.7 g

Ingredients

2 large mangoes, flesh of
1 C. fresh orange juice
2 tbsp. ginger juice
1/8 tsp. ground red pepper
1 pinch cardamom
1/8 tsp. grated nutmeg
1 pinch salt

Directions

1. In a food processor, add the mangoes and orange juice and pulse until pureed.
2. Transfer the mango mixture into a bowl alongside the remaining ingredients and beat until well combined.
3. Transfer the mixture into Popsicle molds evenly.
4. Now, insert 1 Popsicle stick into each mold and place in the freezer until set completely.
5. Carefully, remove the popsicles from molds and enjoy.

ARABIAN CARDAMOM
Spiced Popsicles

Prep Time: 30 min
Total Time: 30 mins

Servings per Recipe: 6
Calories	719.1
Fat	49.0 g
Cholesterol	34.6 mg
Sodium	163.6 mg
Carbohydrates	59.3 g
Protein	16.8 g

Ingredients

2/3-1 C. coconut cream
3 C. whole milk
1 cinnamon stick
1 (14 oz.) cans sweetened condensed milk
1/2 tsp. ground cardamom
1 C. grated unsweetened coconut, lightly toasted

1 tbsp. vanilla extract
1 C. pistachios, toasted and finely chopped

Directions

1. In a pot, add the milk and cinnamon stick and cook until boiling.
2. Set the heat to low heat and cook for about 45 minutes, mixing often.
3. Remove the cinnamon stick and discard it.
4. Stir in the coconut cream and cook for a few minutes, mixing continuously.
5. Remove from the heat and stir in the condensed milk, coconut, pistachios, cardamom and vanilla until well combined.
6. Keep aside to cool completely.
7. Transfer the mixture into Popsicle molds evenly.
8. Now, insert 1 Popsicle stick into each mold and place in the freezer until set completely.
9. Carefully, remove the popsicles from molds and enjoy.

Catalina's
Popsicles Party

🥣 Prep Time: 15 mins
🕐 Total Time: 15 mins

Servings per Recipe: 10
Calories   18.0
Fat   0.1 g
Cholesterol   0.0 mg
Sodium   8.8 mg
Carbohydrates   4.3 g
Protein   0.4 g

Ingredients
6 oz. frozen fruit juice concentrate
3 C. cubed cantaloupes
3/4 C. water
10 paper C.
10 wooden popsicle sticks

Directions
1. In a food processor, add the cantaloupe, juice concentrate and water and pulse until smooth.
2. Transfer the mixture into paper cups evenly and place in the freezer for about 1 hour.
3. Now, insert 1 Popsicle stick into each cup and place in the freezer until set completely.
4. Carefully, remove the popsicles from cups and enjoy.

CALIFORNIA
Paletas

Prep Time: 5 min
Total Time: 6 hr 5 mins

Servings per Recipe: 6
Calories	142
Fat	7.4g
Cholesterol	0mg
Sodium	5mg
Carbohydrates	20.8g
Protein	1g

Ingredients
1/2 C. agave nectar
1 C. warm water
2 avocados, diced
3 tbsp. fresh lime juice
1 pinch salt

Directions
1. In a bowl, add the agave nectar and warm water and mix until well combined.
2. In a food processor, add the agave nectar mixture and remaining ingredients and pulse until smooth.
3. Transfer the mixture into Popsicle molds evenly.
4. Now, insert 1 Popsicle stick into each mold and place in the freezer for about 6 hours.
5. Carefully, remove the popsicles from molds and enjoy.

Summer
Lime and Melon Pops

Prep Time: 10 mins
Total Time: 8 h 45 mins

Servings per Recipe: 6
Calories	58
Fat	0.1g
Cholesterol	0mg
Sodium	59mg
Total Carbohydrates	14.8g
Protein	0.4g

Ingredients
1/2 C. water
1/2 C. white sugar, or to taste
4 C. cubed, seeded watermelon
1 tsp. chopped fresh mint

1/2 lime, juiced
1/2 tsp. grated lime zest
1/4 tsp. salt

Directions
1. In a pot, add the sugar and water and cook until boiling.
2. Cook for about 5 minutes, mixing continuously.
3. Remove from the heat and keep aside to cool.
4. In a food processor, add the sugar syrup and remaining ingredients and pulse until smooth.
5. Transfer the mixture into Popsicle molds evenly.
6. Now, insert 1 Popsicle stick into each mold and place in the freezer for about 2 hours.
7. Carefully, remove the popsicles from molds and enjoy.

LATIN
Rice Paletas

Prep Time: 15 min
Total Time: 2 hr 30 mins

Servings per Recipe: 6
Calories 255
Fat 3.3g
Cholesterol 12mg
Sodium 51mg
Total Carbohydrates 52.6g
Protein 4.5g

Ingredients
2 C. water
1 C. white rice
1 C. white sugar
1 C. sweetened condensed milk
1 C. milk

Directions
1. In a pan, add the rice, sugar and water and cook until boiling.
2. Set the heat to medium-low and cook, covered for about 15-20 minutes.
3. In a bowl, add the cooked rice, milk and condensed milk and mix well.
4. Transfer the mixture into Popsicle molds evenly.
5. Now, insert 1 Popsicle stick into each mold and place in the freezer for about 2 hours.
6. Carefully, remove the popsicles from molds and enjoy.

Little Bear
Popsicles

🥣 Prep Time: 10 mins
🕐 Total Time: 2 h 40 mins

Servings per Recipe: 6
Calories   157
Fat   0.2g
Cholesterol   0mg
Sodium   25mg
Carbohydrates   39.4g
Protein   0.6g

Ingredients

1 (2 liter) bottle lemon-lime soda
1 liter orange juice
1 (5 oz.) bag gummy bears
1 apple, diced

Directions

1. In a bowl, add the orange juice and soda and mix well.
2. In the bottom of paper cups, divide the gummy bears and apple evenly and top with the soda mixture.
3. Now, insert 1 Popsicle stick into each cup and place in the freezer for about 3 hours.
4. Carefully, remove the popsicles from cups and enjoy.

CAMPING
Popsicles

Prep Time: 15 min
Total Time: 3 hr 30 mins

Servings per Recipe: 6
Calories 196
Fat 6g
Cholesterol 21mg
Sodium 348mg
Carbohydrates 31.2g
Protein 4.6g

Ingredients
2 C. cold milk
1 (3.9 oz.) package instant chocolate pudding mix
2 whole graham crackers, crushed
1 1/2 C. vanilla ice cream, softened

Directions
1. In a bowl, add the pudding mix and milk and with an electric mixer, beat until mixture becomes thick.
2. In the bottom of each Popsicle mold, place a thin layer of the cracker crumbs and top with 1/4 C. of the ice cream.
3. Place another layer of cracker crumbs and top with about 1/4 C. of the pudding, followed by the final layer of cracker crumbs.
4. Now, insert 1 Popsicle stick into each mold and place in the freezer for about 3 hours.
5. Carefully, remove the popsicles from molds and enjoy.

London
Morning Popsicles

🥣 Prep Time: 5 mins
🕐 Total Time: 3 h 35 mins

Servings per Recipe: 6
Calories   22
Fat   0g
Cholesterol   0mg
Sodium   3mg
Carbohydrates   6.2g
Protein   0.1g

Ingredients
2 C. boiling water
2 Earl Grey tea bags
2 tbsp. white sugar
1 lime, juiced
6 slices lime

Directions
1. In a pitcher, add the tea bags and top with the boiling water.
2. Keep aside to steep for about 15 minutes.
3. Remove the tea bags from the pitcher.
4. In the pitcher, add the sugar and lime juice and stir to combine well.
5. Keep aside at room temperature to cool.
6. In the bottom of each Popsicle mold, place a lime slice and top with the honey mixture, leaving about 1/4-inch space from the top.
7. Now, insert 1 Popsicle stick into each mold and place in the freezer for about 3-4 hours.
8. Carefully, remove the popsicles from molds and enjoy.

VANILLA
Paletas

Prep Time: 15 min
Total Time: 8 hr 20 mins

Servings per Recipe: 6
Calories   90
Fat   3.5g
Cholesterol   10mg
Sodium   60mg
Total Carbohydrates 14g
Protein   0g

Ingredients

2 C. Almond Breeze Vanilla Cashew blend almond milk
1/4 C. sugar
2 tbsp. cornstarch + 2 tsp. cornstarch
1 tsp. vanilla extract
2 tbsp. coconut oil
3/4 C. fresh raspberries

Directions

1. In a pot, add the almond milk, coconut oil, sugar, cornstarch and vanilla extract and cook until just boiling, mixing continuously.
2. Set the heat to low and cook for about 5 minutes, mixing frequently.
3. Remove from the heat and keep aside to cool, mixing often.
4. After cooling, stir in the raspberries.
5. Transfer the mixture into Popsicle molds evenly.
6. Now, insert 1 Popsicle stick into each mold and place in the freezer overnight.
7. Carefully, remove the popsicles from molds and enjoy.

Fathia's
Favorite Popsicles

🥣 Prep Time: 10 mins
🕐 Total Time: 4 h 10 mins

Servings per Recipe: 6
Calories	211
Fat	11.7g
Cholesterol	21mg
Sodium	171mg
Carbohydrates	24.8g
Protein	4g

Ingredients
1 (8 oz.) package baby carrots
1/2 C. milk
2 tbsp. brown sugar
2 tbsp. white sugar
1 tsp. ground cinnamon
1/2 tsp. ground ginger
1/4 tsp. salt

1/4 tsp. ground nutmeg
2 C. vanilla ice cream
1/2 C. chopped walnuts

Directions
1. In a food processor, add the milk, carrots, sugars, spices and salt and process until smooth.
2. Add the ice cream and process until well combined.
3. Transfer the mixture into Popsicle molds evenly and place in the freezer for about 1 hour.
4. Remove the molds from freezer.
5. Add the walnuts into each mold and mix well.
6. Now, insert 1 Popsicle stick into each mold and place in the freezer for about 4-6 hours.
7. Carefully, remove the popsicles from molds and enjoy.

SWEET COOKIE
Paletas

Prep Time: 10 min
Total Time: 4 hr 10 mins

Servings per Recipe: 6
Calories	426
Fat	35.8g
Cholesterol	114mg
Sodium	111mg
Carbohydrates	24.3g
Protein	4.1g

Ingredients
2 C. heavy whipping cream
1/3 C. sweetened condensed milk
12 chocolate chip cookies

Directions
1. In a bowl, add the condensed milk and heavy cream and mix until blended nicely.
2. In the bottom of each Popsicle mold, place 2 chocolate chip cookies and top with the cream mixture.
3. Now, insert 1 Popsicle stick into each mold and place in the freezer for about 4 hours.
4. Carefully, remove the popsicles from molds and enjoy.

Florida
Cream Popsicles

🥣 Prep Time: 15 mins
🕐 Total Time: 8 h 10 mins

Servings per Recipe: 6
Calories   100
Fat   3,5g
Cholesterol   10mg
Sodium   60mg
Total Carbohydrates 16g
Protein   0g

Ingredients

2 C. Almond Breeze Vanilla almond milk
1/4 C. sugar
2 tbsp. cornstarch + 2 tsp. cornstarch

2 tbsp. coconut oil
1 tsp. vanilla extract
1/4 C. orange juice concentrate, thawed

Directions

1. In a pot, add the almond milk, coconut oil, sugar, cornstarch and vanilla extract and cook until just boiling, mixing continuously.
2. Set the heat to low and cook for about 5 minutes, mixing frequently.
3. Remove from the heat and keep aside to cool, mixing often.
4. Transfer about 2/3 of the almond milk mixture into another bowl with the orange juice concentrate and stir to combine well.
5. Add the remaining almond milk mixture and swirl very lightly.
6. Transfer the mixture into Popsicle molds evenly.
7. Now, insert 1 Popsicle stick into each mold and place in the freezer overnight.
8. Carefully, remove the popsicles from molds and enjoy.

RASPBERRY COCONUT
Popsicles

Prep Time: 10 min
Total Time: 3 hr 10 mins

Servings per Recipe: 6
Calories	206
Fat	17.2g
Cholesterol	0mg
Sodium	11mg
Carbohydrates	15.8g
Protein	2.7g

Ingredients
1 (13.5 oz.) can full-fat coconut milk
5 tbsp. cocoa powder
1/4 C. white sugar
1/4 C. fresh raspberries
1/4 tsp. almond extract

Directions
1. In a food processor, add all the ingredients and pulse until smooth.
2. Transfer the mixture into disposable cups evenly.
3. Now, insert 1 Popsicle stick into each cup and place in the freezer for about 3 hours.
4. Carefully, remove the popsicles from molds and enjoy.

Leafy
Greek Popsicles

🥄 Prep Time: 10 mins
🕐 Total Time: 2 h 10 mins

Servings per Recipe: 6
Calories   103
Fat   2.8g
Cholesterol   7mg
Sodium   38mg
Carbohydrates   17.8g
Protein   3.2g

Ingredients

1 C. milk
1 C. frozen blueberries
1 C. frozen cherries
1/2 C. Greek yogurt

1/2 C. frozen chopped spinach, thawed and drained
3 tbsp. honey

Directions

1. In a food processor, add all the ingredients and pulse until smooth.
2. Transfer the mixture into Popsicle molds evenly.
3. Now, insert 1 Popsicle stick into each mold and place in the freezer for about 2 hours.
4. Carefully, remove the popsicles from molds and enjoy.

BLUEBERRY
Summer Popsicles

 Prep Time: 5 min

Total Time: 2 hr 5 mins

Servings per Recipe: 8

Calories	37 kcal
Fat	0 g
Carbohydrates	8.4g
Protein	0.9 g
Cholesterol	< 1 mg
Sodium	< 15 mg

Ingredients
1 C. Ocean Spray(R) Blueberry Juice Cocktail
1 C. Ocean Spray(R) Fresh Blueberries,
cleaned and rinsed

1 (6 oz.) container fat-free vanilla yogurt
8 wooden craft sticks

Directions
1. In a blender, add all the ingredients and pulse on high speed till smooth.
2. Transfer the mixture into 8 (2.5-3 oz.)Frozen pop molds.
3. Insert the craft sticks and freeze for about 2 hours.
4. Just before serving, dip the outsides of molds into warm water to loosen.

Tropical
Popsicles

🥣 Prep Time: 15 mins
🕐 Total Time: 2 h 15 mins

Servings per Recipe: 6
Calories   163.9
Fat   0.4g
Cholesterol   0.0mg
Sodium   1.4mg
Carbohydrates   41.7g
Protein   0.9g

Ingredients

pulp of 2 ripe medium-size mangoes
3/4 C. sugar
water
3/4 C. cracked ice

Directions

1. Get a food blender: Combine in it all the ingredients. Blend them smooth.
2. Spoon the mix into 2 popsicle molds. Freeze them for 3 h.
3. Serve your popsicles.
4. Enjoy.

FRUIT MEDLEY
Autumn Popsicles

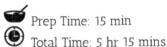

Prep Time: 15 min
Total Time: 5 hr 15 mins

Servings per Recipe: 8
Calories	83 kcal
Fat	1.1 g
Cholesterol	15.8g
Sodium	3.5 g
Carbohydrates	4 mg
Protein	43 mg

Ingredients
2 C. fresh blueberries, raspberries,
strawberries and sliced bananas, mixed
2 C. plain or vanilla yogurt
1/4 C. white sugar
8 small paper C.
8 popsicle sticks

Directions
1. Add the following to the bowl of a food processor: sugar, blueberries, yogurt, raspberries, bananas, and strawberries. Puree the mix completely. Divide the mix between disposable C. then place a covering of plastic on each C.
2. Place a stick into each C. then place everything in the freezer overnight.
3. Enjoy.